MW01519967

THE JOY OF BECOMING GOD

The Joy of Becoming God

First Printed in the United States by
Vervante.

ISBN: 978-0-9817703-7-6

www.soulpowermagic.com

**You can contact the author at
vish@vish-writer.com. You
can also reach him at his US number at
2138142680.**

Also by Sri Vishwanath

1) **Shakti** : Revealed- How You Can Feel Great In Sixty Seconds Flat

2) **Zero Effort** : How To Achieve Big Breakthroughs In Your Life In Less Than 30 days Flat

3) **Know" That One Thing"** - The Spiritual Guide That Been 5500 years in the making. Discover The Quickest and surest path to God...

4) **Shraddha**- Everything You Wanted To Know Above Love And God

5) **No-Nonsense Meditation –** What The Greatest Wise Men & Women Knew About Human Consciousness That You Are Not Aware Of.

6) **The Story of Nachiketa** – How A Little Boy Conquered Death By Meditating On A Force Superior to Death

7) **Give Up --- Everything That You Love.** 24 Simple Mind Exercises That Great Men & Women Effectively Use Every Single Day

8) **Shiva**- The Story of How God Mentored An Ordinary Man To Experience Extraordinary Levels of Super Consciousness In A Single Game Of Dice.

Dedication

TO LORD KRISHNA, SRI RAMAKRISHNA,
SWAMI VIVEKANANDA & SHARADA DEVI

I BECOME WHAT I SEE IN MYSELF. ALL THAT THOUGHT SUGGESTS TO ME, I CAN DO, ALL THAT THOUGHT REVEALS IN ME, I CAN BECOME. THIS SHOULD BE MAN'S UNSHAKABLE FAITH IN HIMSELF, BECAUSE GOD DWELLS IN HIM.

SRI AUROBINDO

IF THERE IS GOD, WE MUST SEE HIM; IF THERE IS A SOUL, WE MUST PERCEIVE IT; OTHERWISE IT IS BETTER NOT TO BELIEVE. IT IS BETTER TO BE AN OUTSPOKEN ATHEIST THAN A HYPOCRITE.

SWAMI VIVEKANANDA

It was the 14th of January 1806, a very special day which would be remembered in the history of mankind. Though it was one a.m. midnight, close to a thousand people had turned up outside the forest area of Mariranga, in North-east India. Something miraculous was going to happen that day, something so unusual that it had never happened before and probably would never occur again for a long time to come.......

The forest area was very dense. No one had ever dared to venture into it. Villagers believed that three wild beasts roamed inside, a leopard, a tiger, and a lion. But this day was special... The forest had a giant gate which prohibited anyone from entering. The gatekeeper, Vignesh, had his small tent outside the forest gate where he lived.

A strange and powerful light had

woken up the whole village. The villagers in the middle of the night scrambled out of their beds to watch this light......

Standing outside the gates of the forest they could see a resplendent light bathing the trees and dense bush of the forest. Three of the most revered men in the history of the world were waving to them.

Many villagers jumped and danced with joy. Tears of happiness flowed, while others stood speechless.... It was the most beautiful moment on earth. All the villagers felt blessed to witness this spectacle....

The villagers had members from all faiths. Some were Hindus, some Christians, and some Muslims. No one could believe their eyes. But the images of the three men outlined sharply in the strong light were so clear. It seemed unbelievable to the villagers but there were Lord Krishna, Jesus and Mohammed in flesh and blood!

The three great religious leaders waved to the crowd and then motioned the men and women to approach closer. But the villagers were fearful of the forest and the dangerous beasts. They would have to cross the forest to meet these great men of faith.

Why should such inspiring religious figures descend to this tiny village and in human form? Yet the grandeur of their personalities could be seen and experienced by everyone in the crowd. Lord Krishna, Jesus and Mohammed in human form!

The scene was nothing short of the most chaotic and yet the most wonderful moment in history. Here in their simple community, the villagers realized was a marvelous opportunity to meet three of the most venerated figures of three of the world's greatest religions. But there was still the hurdle of passing through the forest. Though the religious leaders continued to smile and wave to the villagers, none of them moved forward, still fearful of being attacked by the wild animals.

Then something very strange happened.... A beautiful and refreshing voice was heard from within the forest, with a command to the gatekeeper: "Vignesh, go back to your tent. Nobody from the crowd will follow you. Inside the tent, you will see a diamond shaped treasure box containing a small note. Open the box, read the note three times, and then swallow the small piece of paper. You have to whisper what I have written in that note into the ear of every person who wants to see us...They would then be able to cross over the forest without any problem and meet us. However, every one who wants to meet us has to come alone."

The voice echoed twice and then disappeared. The crowd went frantic and did not know what to do. Some screamed, while others laughed. A few knelt in prayer.

Meanwhile Vignesh, as dutiful as ever, went back to his small tent. As instructed he opened the note, read it three times, and then swallowed it.

A mad rush ensued outside the tent the moment he came out. Everyone was desperate to see what was written in that note. Some villagers even forcibly opening his mouth to retrieve the note ......

A voice from the forest came back again "Don't touch him. Listen to what he says."

Everyone moved away in awe of the God-like voice.

Vignesh went back to the forest gate. The atmosphere was electrifying. What should he say? The light now seemed even more powerful than before. Human eyes, Vignesh thought, could not visualize this heavenly spectacle. The vision of these great men was grander, majestic and more blissful than any human being had ever seen. Words and picture could perhaps never capture the moment....

Vignesh raised his hand and voice in a gentle yet commanding manner. "I have very exciting news for all of you. Each of you can experience God through contact with the great man from your own religion. You have an opportunity to be with God today."

Many villagers screamed, rolled in the ground with ecstasy, and beat their chest. The joy in the faces of a thousand people was surely unparalleled in the history of the world. A chance to be with God, experience Him face to face!! Blessed was he, Vignesh thought, who saw all this...

Vignesh yelled. "Stop all this. There are three rules which you have to follow. So listen:

One, everyone, who wants to experience God, will have to cross this dense forest.

Two, each one of you must go alone. I will whisper a very special message given by God into your ears before I open the forest gates for you. You have to follow that message at any cost. This will help you cross the forest. The beasts will not kill you and you will be able to come before your religious leader if you strictly follow the message."

Vignesh paused a moment to let his words sink in. Finally, he went on, "Once you have lined up to meet God you cannot back up. You cannot get out of the line if you see any of your fellow villagers being killed by the wild animals because they haven't followed the instructions. .If anyone backs up these religious leaders will disappear and the whole village would be destroyed. Now I request everyone who is interested in experiencing God to step forward,"

A strange silence ensued. No one

moved... Everyone stood still, transfixed at first by the magnificence of the religious figures and the extraordinary chance to have such an encounter with God.

But then they began to have doubts. Why would God want them to cross the forest to meet Him? Why couldn't the Lord grant them a personal audience right in their village and outside the dangers of the forest? However, none had the courage to ask this question to God.

Vignesh raised his hand "I will count to ten.... if no one turns up these great men will disappear and never come back again. I urge everyone not to miss this opportunity."

He started counting. One, two, three, four, five, six...

One man from the crowd raised his hand and came forward

But Vignesh kept counting. Seven, eight....

A woman stepped out of the crowd with a courageous expression on her face.

And still Vignesh finished counting. Nine, ten...

A youth joined the first two in front of the others.

Everyone else cheered these three individuals. The shouting and chanting began. The excitement returned back. Many from the crowd went and congratulated these three people for their bravery.

The trio lined up 50 metres near the forest gate. The chanting and roar from the crowds became deafening. What would happen to these three people, Vignesh wondered? Would they be able to see God? ...

"Come over, Rahul," Vignesh said, summoning the first man.

A thunderous applause rang out for Rahul, a Hindu by religion, as he walked the fifty-meter distance towards the main forest gate.

Vignesh raised his hand for quiet. The villagers were quick to co-operate. The silence returned. Leaning closely towards Rahul, Vignesh whispered those mystical words into his ears. He then gave him his blessing and opened the forest gate...

The crowd murmured with anticipation and curiosity over what would happen to Rahul.

Would he succeed in reaching the religious leader? The voice was boisterous....

The forest had three hundred acres of land. It was believed that a leopard wandered around in the first hundred acres of land. A white Siberian tiger was said to have been spotted in the next hundred acres. A ferocious African lion was believed to roam the last hundred acres. Rahul had to cross this entire stretch before he confronted Lord Krishna.

People outside the forest remained in a state of great excitement and apprehension, with no way of knowing of Rahul's fate. Would he be eaten or actually experience God through Krishna? The atmosphere was very tense, and everyone prayed for Rahul. For the first time the villagers stood united.... They wanted from the bottom of their hearts that Rahul should realize God. A wonderful glow had spread across the whole village. The powerful light and the magnificence of the religious figures continued to hold the crowd spellbound.

Thirty minutes passed by and there was no noise. Another thirty minutes passed by. Then, a gentle voice echoed through the forest..."Rahul did not want to meet God. He was killed by the leopard."

A thousand hearts sank like one in the soft mud. Their faces dropped. They all loved Rahul, who was gone... forever. The person who stood in flesh and blood an hour back had disappeared into ether....

" Roseline, its your turn. Come forward" Vignesh ordered the woman. Roseline, seeing the fate of

Rahul, trembled with fear. The confidence in her an hour back was nowhere to be seen. Now she looked like a sacrificial lamb walking those fifty steps towards the front of the main gate. Poor woman, Vignesh thought! She had no choice. She could not go back. If she did the men of faith would disappear and the whole village would be destroyed.

Vignesh hugged Roseline, a Christian by birth, and prayed that she would be successful. He leaned forward towards her and whispered those mystical words again...

"I want all of you to give Roseline a thunderous applause" Vignesh then told the villagers.

The entire assembly rose to their feet once again and gave her a standing ovation. They all blessed her and shouted their best wishes. Hope had returned back to the crowd... They had something to cheer about. The gates were flung open and Roseline was allowed to go inside...

The gates were shut and the villagers sat down and prayed ... Each person, Vignesh thought, wanted Roseline to realize God in their own way. Their collective intent, visible in their faces, was genuine. Their voices were choked with emotion. The village was truly blessed with the vision of a divine image....

During all this commotion, the three men of God were calm. Standing with a serene presence, their visages matched the magnificence of the blue sky and the brilliance of the sun. Was all this real or was it a trick of the human mind, some villagers still wondered?

An hour passed by with Roseline in the forest. Then another hour ended. The villagers became increasingly restless. They could not wait to listen to the voice from the forest again.

"First the good news" came the deep-sounding words that wafted over the trees like a wind. "Roseline did manage to cross over the first hundred acres. She passed by the leopard safely"

There was a loud cheer. The crowd went wild.

The voice continued. ......"Now the bad news..." Roseline too was not keen enough to encounter God. She did not follow the second instruction given to her. The tiger has killed her"

The noise of the crowd died. Many shouted angry accusations back towards the voice. Some villagers pleaded to God to stop the entire process. The crowd had enough of all this. Others then appealed to Vignesh to stop Rahim, the youth, from entering the forest. They did not want him to also die.

Still the villagers were consumed by curiosity and wanted to know what were the instructions the voice had passed to Vignesh. They asked Vignesh not to send Rahim into the forest, but the gatekeeper felt compelled to follow His instructions.

As if imbued with divine wisdom, Vignesh said, "Every action of God has a purpose and meaning behind it which we as human doings don't understand at times."

The villagers listened with respect

and then talked among themselves. Vignesh interrupted their deliberations and said, "Understand that if Rahim doesn't return I'll go myself into the forest."

Rahim, in all this confusion, was like a pawn in the hands of the crowd.

"Please come here, Rahim" Vignesh requested. Vignesh kissed Rahim on his forehead, applied the holy ash, and repeated those mystical words into Rahim's ear. He wished him good luck.

Rahim, a devout Muslim, took some steps toward the forest but then hesitated. As if there were no hope for the lad, many villagers were in tears. The gates were thrown open. Rahim entered the forest and the gates were shut. A sepulchral silence came over the villagers as if they were already mourning Rahim's death...

The men of God were still waving towards the villagers urging more of them to come before them. Though the brilliant light emanating from the figures of God shone with even greater intensity, the villagers' fear of the forest had become even stronger due to the deaths of Rahul and Roseline.

Why would anyone not allow the brilliance of God to shine over them? Why would they deny permission to God to enter into their body and mind because of two bad events, thought Vignesh?

Two hours passed by with no information about Rahim.

"This time I have very good news for you" came the soothing voice from the forest. "Rahim has tamed the leopard and the tiger and is on his way towards the last hundred acres."

The crowd was once again alive. The villagers rejoiced as if a dead child was reborn. Their joy was unparalleled, and they prayed with the utmost devotion for Rahim.

Another hour passed by.... The chanting increased as their belief in Rahim's welfare becoming stronger by the moment. Their despair, two hours back, had now given rise to hope. It is sometimes so strange, Vignesh thought, how human beings give up so easily and how just two measures of success could lift them from a communal depression.

Then came the voice again....

"Rahim has failed in the last hurdle. He was eaten by the lion.

He was a fool not to follow the third instruction..."

The crowd was furious and shouted curses while throwing stones at the forest. They were convinced that the figures they saw in the forest were not representatives of God. God, they cried to one another, wouldn't kill three innocent people.

In all this commotion Vignesh was quiet. He believed in God and had complete faith in Him. He bowed towards the three religious figures, kissed the ground, and prayed for several moments. He then stood; ready to fulfill his promise...

As Vignesh flung open the gates he walked with a steady gait, making sure he didn't look like a sacrificial lamb. Before the crowd could realize it he had entered into the forest...

By now the crowd's mood had simmered down. Many of them felt bad about their behaviour. In the silence of their hearts they applauded the boldness of Vignesh. The morning sun had already come up but the brilliance of Krishna, Jesus and Mohammed outshone even the rays of the sun.

In the last six hours, it seemed to the villagers, that everyone had lost complete faith in God. When invisible God was not questioned for centuries, but now a visible representation of God in human form could not survive even for six hours. Why is this so, they each asked themselves? Did we always want God to remain hidden in memory and be *apart* from us instead of being *a part* of us? Why didn't we allow permission to God to take control of ourselves?

Two and half hours more had now passed by....

"Vignesh is on his way to meet us," the voice sounded again from deep within the forest. "He has humbled the leopard, and the tiger. He has also crossed half the distance of the last hundred acres. I want you to pray for him with utmost devotion."

A cheer had returned back to the crowd, though some thought God was just being clever. He knew no one would pray for Him so he urged the villages to pray for Vignesh. They were not overjoyed but there was a huge hope factor. The eight hours of adventure was heading for an exciting climax. Everyone in the crowd closed their eyes, chanted a silent prayer, and remained in that position for what seemed like an eternity. It was the most wondrous moment in their lives. A thousand people were praying with complete submission to the representatives of three faiths.

And lo and behold! A great resolution which everyone wanted happened. A circle of golden faith, like a shining mist, could be literally seen rising and moving towards the forest. The power of belief for the first time could be seen physically advancing and the villagers felt a humble appreciation of the glorious and uplifting sight.. Some villagers went into a trance. Many started dancing with joy with others now singing praises of the Lord. Faith had jumped back on their shoulders...

From a distance everyone could see the resplendent mist of faith advancing deeper into the forest. It was as if the mist acted as a shield of energy to protect Vignesh from the beasts.

The entire crowd continued to celebrate as if they didn't feel the need to wait for the voice to speak again. They knew that nothing could stop Vignesh from meeting God...

And then the moment which everyone was waiting for came. A familiar voice resounded from the interior of the forest, but this time it was the voice of Vignesh. "I have arrived safely. I am in the company of God..."

Everyone looked in the direction of the forest but there was no way one could differentiate between Vignesh, Krishna, Jesus, and Mohammed. They all resembled the pure consciousness, the one force which makes up every form in this world. The crowd was wildly celebrating as if demonstrating the enormous power of faith. Each person in the crowd felt as if they had somehow experienced the presence of God.

Moments of Joy! Unparalleled in history. It was a live demonstration of the greatest power within human beings at work. The flesh being ripped apart and the heart exposed, a soul moving. Even an atheist would be convinced of the greatness of the soul.

But then, just as suddenly as they had appeared, the figures of God disappeared and Vignesh was back at the forest gate

The crowd could not control themselves. They fell at his feet, and many embraced him. He was completely mobbed and had no clue of what was happening. He had a big bag in his hands. Before he could speak they snatched the bag from him and ripped it open. In it was a magnificent idol of Lord Krishna, a cross of Jesus, and a copy of the Quran, the holy book of the Muslims.

Vignesh wanted to declare what God had instructed him to tell his fellow villagers, but the crowd was too boisterous. They kissed the idol, the cross, and the Quran.

The Hindus then snatched the idol of Krishna from him, and vowed to build a temple at the forest gate in his honor.

The Christians took the cross with them and prayed to Jesus, promising to build a church in the village.

The Muslims preserved the Quran and also vowed to build a big mosque in the village.

None of the villagers thought to ask what God had written in the note he gave to Vignesh.

Vignesh had managed to see God when others could not. He wanted to share all this with everyone but they were all busy with their plans for worshipping in their temples, churches and mosques. Left alone, he took four sheets of paper. In the first sheet, he wrote the secret message God had asked him to whisper in the trio's ears, and in the other three he wrote everything that was revealed to him after he crossed the forest. He placed these notes in a treasure box inside his hut. With a last look at the village he opened the gate and disappeared into the forest...

For a long time the notes remained untouched in the treasure box, but many years later, after Vignesh and all the other villagers were no longer alive, a stranger visiting the village to see the famous three places of worship so close together at the edge of the forest, found them. He read the contents and was mystified until a descendent of one of the villagers explained the meaning. Copies of the notes were then placed in the temple, church, and mosque. The first note read:

There is no leopard, tiger or lion in the forest. You created these three beasts in your mind.

The leopard that you think which exists in the first hundred acres of the land is nothing but the element of "fear" which is present in your mind.

The Siberian tiger that you think exists in the next hundred acres represents nothing but the element of "insecurity of your future life."

The man-eating lion which you think roams in the last hundred acres of the forest is nothing but the factor of "doubt" in believing your own inner voice.

Drop these three things from your mind before you enter the forest. FEAR, INSECURITY ABOUT YOUR FUTURE, AND

DOUBT IN YOUR INNER VOICE only exist in your mind. They were never real. You magnified them and thus created the danger of the wild beasts.

I say to you, as the Lord of the three worlds that there is no leopard, tiger and lion in the forest. Before you enter the forest of your mind to realize me I want you to drop fear, insecurity about your future, and doubt from your mind. You have to remove all of them from your mind before you enter into the forest. Even if one of them remains you will not be able to see Me. So my dear child, I wish you all the best and I will wait eagerly to welcome you"

INSPIRED BY GOD

COUNTERSIGNED BY YOUR INNER VOICE

Vignesh had written something even more interesting in the other three sheets of paper.

"I wanted to tell everyone in the village why Rahul, Roseline and Rahim could not see God. God had caged all the three beasts in the forests so they would not harm the true seeker. However, if anyone did not follow the instructions given to them the doors of the cage would be thrown open.

Strange as it may sound, Rahul could not believe the statements of God and he was killed by the leopard. Did the leopard really kill him? Yes.

If Rahul had dropped fear from his mind the leopard would not have harmed him. Rahul kept the door of fear open in his mind and the leopard jumped out of the cage and ate him.-

Fear of dying, fear of failure, and fear of embarrassment are not created by our own mind. These thoughts can never be our own thoughts. How can the brain which God gifted you with have such impurities? As you started living your life you sensed fear and nourished fears which grew into a wild beast which could frighten you any time. These fears became the leopard.

Roseline was a very bold woman. She truly believed in God's words. She did drop fear, insecurity and doubt at the forest gate. However, as she passed the first hundred acres of land she saw the leopard in the cage. She got terribly frightened and started running in the forest. She completely forgot about the instructions given by God and was soon lost. Seizing this opportunity, the two beasts of insecurity and doubt again jumped back into her mind. She was able to cross the first hundred acres of land but the tiger ate her.

When you put on the lights, darkness disappears but how far does it go.... not too far away waiting for a chance to come back... The moment you think you are secure the darkness of insecurity strikes back. At what *point* can you really say that you are secured? If you ask your mind to take you to that *point it* would always be a future *point. At a* later date when you reach that *future point* and ask your mind the same question, it would steer you again to a farther *future point.*

The mind is the creator of that future *point* called insecurity. How can the mind which itself is a creator of insecurity also teach you about security? Insecurity about money, health and relationships exists in the present and not in the future. You allowed the fear of insecurity to drift into the future and you became its prey for decades. The fear of insecurity took the form of a tiger.

Rahim was a gutsy lad. He knew

Rahul and Roseline were killed but his faith in God was total. He believed that if Allah gave birth to him, Allah would also take care of him. So he walked through the forest with determination. He crossed the first hundred acres without any fear. He saw the leopard in a cage but he smiled. His confidence grew. He knew Allah was taking care of him. The next hundred acres were not difficult at all. He spotted the tiger who was caged and felt very happy as he knew very soon he would be in Allah's presence. Half way through the last hundred acres of land Rahim was still confidently walking. However, as he walked the final distance he could no longer see the lion in the cage.

Where could the lion be, he wondered?

Would the lion attack him from behind?

Would he have to fight the lion?

As he inched his way towards the end of the last hundred acres all these thoughts had completely taken over him. He doubted his own inner voice. He believed in Allah but the belief was pale and shallow compared to the mad rush of fears which had taken over him.

Rahim had only to walk forward but he was looking back and sideways fearing that the lion might attack him. For those brief moments Rahim doubted the words of Allah; and suddenly a beast leaped upon him from behind and killed him. He was destroyed by the wild beast created by his own mind. Rahim made one major mistake. He was almost there but could not make that final leap.

Doubt in your own inner voice is the deadliest of beasts residing within you. It is one of the strange things that we do not believe God but we believe fear and insecurity about our future. We accept things our mind perceives which in reality do not exist. When we can believe all these things which we have never seen, which are nothing but creations of our mind, why do we have problems believing God? Why do we doubt Him? Why do we doubt our inner voice which is nothing but the voice of God speaking through us? Why do we have problems allowing the higher force within us to guide us? You doubted the brilliance of your higher self and allowed your mind to build a palace of wants for yourself. A palace where your desires were the king and you were the slave. You doubted your inner voice and it created in you the fear of losing everything which you perhaps never ever wanted in the first place. This fear took the form of a lion.

I had no clue of what had happened to Rahul, Roseline, and Rahim. God told me of their fate only later after I met Him. I want to tell you that I had no courage to meet God. That is the reason God chose me to whisper His secret message in the ears of all those who were genuinely interested in meeting Him. I was short of both courage and confidence.

It was God's will maybe that He allowed me to experience Him. I knew right from the start that I would not be able to cross this forest alone when I had so little courage. So when I kissed the ground and knelt down I completely submitted myself to God. I asked God to accompany me on this difficult journey.

I gave permission to God to take control over my mind and body. I knew that with the powers of my mind I would not be able to drop fear, insecurity and doubt. So I allowed the spirit of God to enter me. This was no blind belief but I simply allowed a greater force which runs this universe to take charge over me.

This is how I did it. Before I gave permission to God to enter my mind I gave permission to myself to completely destroy my old rusted mind. All along my life I was holding a glass full of muddy water and pleading to the universe to fill it with fresh water. How could that possibly happen? All I needed to do was to empty this glass of muddy water to allow the fresh water to be filled in. That day I was left with no option. I had to let go of my old blighted or corroded mind to give way to that magnificent brain which could literally hand over to me anything I want.

In those tense moments I managed to do what I could not do for two decades. I gathered sufficient courage to let go of my old befuddled brain and replace it with the marvelous brain of God.

It was strange why I never valued my mind before. I gave permission to all the stinking and miserable thoughts to enter into my consciousness. I used to keep all my money in a bank and took great care of my money. But I did not accord the same value to my mind. I did not think that my mind was the greatest and wealthiest resource in my life.

I saw all the things I should not have paid any attention to. I spoke on all subjects, events, and persons which made no difference to the quotient of happiness within me. Over the years I accumulated tons of garbage. I kept a wastebasket in my tent but I did not buy one for all the junk thoughts which had accumulated in my mind. These thoughts were decaying but I paid little attention. Whenever someone asked me something, I used to go to that rusty mind filled with poor thoughts to give an answer. I was searching for a golden egg in a waste basket.

We think that the problem lies in *filling* the mind with fresh water but the real problem lies in allowing ourselves to *empty* the muddy water from the mind. The fresh water was always waiting there to be *filled*. I realized this awakening in those split seconds....

I also knew that to empty my misused mind and make it free of all inferior thoughts would take me at least five years of meditation and silence. But I had no time.... I had to get a new brain in a few minutes. So as my head touched the ground I asked God, what I should do? And the answer was clear to me as He felt His spirit in me.

'Submit yourself completely to Me'

And so I submitted myself completely to Him at that moment. It was the best thing to happen to me. There was no way in the world that I could meet God with my brain. I repeat, there was no way I could reach Him with my line of thinking.

It was the two wisest things I did in my life. First, to give permission to myself to destroy my old mind, and second, to allow God and grant him permission to take control of my mind and body. How could anyone fail with a new brain life-changing surging in their mind?

My brain was light and there were no thoughts in it. It was a new-born brain. I opened the forest gate with the anxiety of a child who is desperate to meet his mother. I ran with the delight of the child wanting to run into his mother's arms. As I ran the leopard, tiger and lion seemed like pussycats waving to me. Which mother has denied permission to a child wanting to meet him?

There was one more thing which happened during the time I was running inside the forest. The villagers had also destroyed their old minds and allowed the inner force within them to expand. The mist of faith which everyone saw was no miracle. There are no miracles in life. No wise men or women would dare use that word miracle. Miracles or the supernatural are nothing but the nature of things which we have not yet experienced or attained or do not yet know or the means of which we have not yet conquered.

But when I returned from the forest the villagers were eager to have their old minds back. They pounced on me to regain their minds. They wanted the idol, the cross, and the Quran. They were satisfied with the momentary glimpse of the inner beauty which they had experienced but they had no intention of holding on to that thread which could have taken them all the way to permanent happiness. What a big mistake!

I have one more confession to make. I did not see Lord Krishna, Jesus, or Mohammed.

God with form and God without form are like ice and water. When water freezes into ice it has form. When the same ice is melted into water, all form is lost. The form that we see from a distance gives way to something more realistic when we come close to it. When I crossed the three hundred acres of land I had conquered the three beasts of fear, insecurity and doubt. When I came to the other side of the forest I got more than what I wanted. I was given an opportunity to touch *that thing* in me which was nothing but pure gold. Everything else seemed unreal for me from that point on ….the leopard, tiger, lion and many more dangers. I was given this reward not by a religious leader in human form but by a higher force within me for driving away the three beasts from my mind.

I became the king of my own kingdom, the kingdom called the mind. Before I allowed myself to crown me as the king of the entire kingdom, I captured my own mind bit by bit. First I conquered fear, then I conquered insecurity, and finally I gobbled up doubt. The impurities of the external world have no place in my kingdom. I had allowed them to reign as my ruler for decades. The external world now has to take permission from me the *real sovereign* to enter.

The external world exists *outside* where it should be and not *inside* where it should never have been.

When I was running like a child in the forest I cried with tears of joy over the explicit joy of meeting the divine sculptor who had created me. Did I encounter any pain, suffering, or fear? No way? How could I? I had given way to my mind and body. All the pain and suffering which exists in the world exists in the mind and body. When I gave permission to God to take over my mind and body, I was given *that thing* to hold on to, which was more real than my mind and body. That thread, catching hold of which like a spider moving towards the center, I crawled towards God with the name of Krishna in my lips. When I reached the other end of the forest the name of Krishna vanished and I felt the extraordinary power of having the keys to my own fear-free world.

When I was the gatekeeper I saw

myself in everything that my eyes saw, in everything that I thought, in every act that I performed. When I had conquered the three beasts, *my-self* had given way to the *real self* which was masked by my own body and thoughts. I am now the master of my mind. When these eyes *see* an individual it does not see the surface of the mind and body it sees something deeper, *that thing* which it can connect to very easily. We feel that the front door of every human being is the mind and the body, but I had found the keys to that secret door which exists in every one of us. I am the king of my kingdom and the servant of every other kingdom which respects my kingdom. No act seems unworthy to me for everything that I touch is pure gold.

God is simple, everything else is complex. He wants us to realize mastery over our beings through Him. He wants us to be the king of our own kingdom....

I had found *that thing* in me which is my real self. I allowed myself to become the God of my own being and so I became...."

Vignesh
Son of the Lord